# SOME WORDS HELP, SOME WORDS HURT

ELSPETH CAMPBELL MURPHY
ILLUSTRATED BY SUSAN MORRIS

Chariot Books
David C. Cook Publishing Co.

Chariot Books is an imprint of David C. Cook Publishing Co.
David C. Cook Publishing Co., Elgin, Illinois 60120
David C. Cook Publishing Co., Weston, Ontario

SOME WORDS HELP, SOME WORDS HURT


Illustrated by Sue Morris; book and cover design by Marilyn Baridon

First Printing, 1988
Printed in Singapore
93 92 91 90 89 88 5 4 3 2 1

**Library of Congress Cataloging-in-Publication Data**
Murphy, Elspeth Campbell.
Some words help, some words hurt.
(Proverbs to grow on)
Summary: In describing Valentine Day at school, a child points out how words can make things worse or better and it is important to use words kindly.
1. Conversation—Juvenile literature. 2. Kindness—Juvenile literature. 3. Children—Conduct of life. 4. Bible. O.T. Proverbs—Juvenile literature. [1. Conduct of life. 2. Bible. O.T. Proverbs]
I. Morris, Susan, ill. II. Title. III. Series: Murphy, Elspeth, Campbell. Proverbs to grow on.
BJ2121.M87 1988 177 87-38205
ISBN 1-55513-164-6

When I woke up this morning, God,
I couldn't make a sound!
My throat didn't hurt,
and I didn't have a fever.
I just couldn't talk—*laryngitis*!
I didn't want to miss the
valentine party at school,
so my mother let me go.

My mother wrote a note to my teacher,
explaining what was wrong with me.
My teacher kind of laughed
when she read the note.
That's because usually
I'm one of the *talkiest* kids in the class.
My teacher is always telling me
to be quiet and listen.

PROVERBS
17:27

*Someone who is sure of himself does not talk all the time. People who stay calm have real insight.*

Today, listening was all I could do.
So I paid attention
to the words going on around me.
And guess what I figured out, God.
Some words help.
And some words hurt.

It's like when this girl in my class
started crying because she thought she
had left her bag of valentines at home.
One kid said to her,
"Oh, you're *so dumb*!
Now you won't have any valentines
to pass out.
And nobody should give any to *you*!"

PROVERBS
11:12

*It is foolish to speak scornfully of others.
If you are smart, you will keep quiet.*

But another kid said,
"Maybe you just got your valentine bag
mixed up with your lunch sack.
If you want,
I'll help you look."

**PROVERBS 12:25**

*An anxious heart weighs a man down,
but a kind word cheers him up.*

And that's exactly what had happened,
God.
So everything turned out OK.
But it's funny how one person's words
made things worse.
And another person's words
made things better.

PROVERBS
12:18

*Reckless words pierce like a sword, but*
*the tongue of the wise brings healing.*

When it was time for the party,
the boy who was passing out
the cupcakes
accidentally skipped a whole bunch of kids.
They were pretty mad,
and they yelled, "Hey, what about us?"

Then the boy with the cupcakes said,
"Oops! Sorry!"
And he was so nice about it,
that those kids didn't stay mad at him.
But they probably would have gotten
even madder
if he had said something mean—
right, God?

**PROVERBS 15:1**

*A gentle answer turns away wrath, but a harsh word stirs up anger.*

I like it when words come out right.
My teacher put this valentine puzzle
on the board,
and suddenly I knew the answer.
Of course, I couldn't talk,
so my teacher let me write in the blanks.
And my answer fit perfectly.
And that's the way it is
when a person says
the right thing
at the right time.
The words just fit.

PROVERBS
15:23

*What a joy it is to find just the right word for the right occasion!*

You know what, God?
I decided that words are one reason
I like getting valentines so much—
because hearing nice words
makes you feel good.
It's sort of like getting something
good to eat.

PROVERBS
16:24

*Pleasant words are a honeycomb, sweet to the soul and healing to the bones.*

This was a very nice day, God—
even though I had to be quiet
the whole time.
Maybe tomorrow I will get my voice back.
I will probably still be
a talky kind of person.
Only—I really will try to listen more.
And when I do talk—
I want to say *good* things!

**PROVERBS**
**10:32**

*Righteous people know the kind thing to say, but the wicked are always saying things that hurt.*

You know why, God?
Because then I will
be trying to copy you!

**PROVERBS 30:5**

*Every word of God is flawless; he is a shield to those who take refuge in him.*